THE SHORT AND
BLOODY
HISTORY
OF
GHOSTS

John Farman

THE SHORT AND BLOODY HISTORY OF GHOSTS

Red Fox

A Red Fox Book

Published by Random House Children's Books
20 Vauxhall Bridge Road, London SW1V 2SA

A division of The Random House Group Ltd
London Melbourne Sydney Auckland
Johannesburg and agencies throughout the world

Copyright © John Farman 2001

1 3 5 7 9 10 8 6 4 2

First published in Great Britain by
Red Fox Children's Books 2001

Printed and bound in Great Britain by
Bookmarque Ltd, Croydon, Surrey

Papers used by Random House Group Ltd are natural,
recyclable products made from wood grown in sustainable forests.
The manufacturing processes conform to the
environmental regulations of the country of origins.

The Random House Group Limited Reg. No. 954009

www.randomhouse.co.uk

ISBN 0 09 941725 1

CONTENTS

To all ghosts everywhere

HOW TO BE A GHOST

Ever fancied being a ghost? I know it sounds a bit morbid, but I have. Think of the mischief you could get up to – floating around like the Invisible Man (or Woman), getting into movies free, driving around in flash cars, or living in posh places like Buckingham Palace. Even better you could go around late at night scaring the wits out of people you didn't like and, best of all, you wouldn't have to do boring things like eating, drinking, washing or going to the lav. But what exactly is a ghost and what do you have to do to become one?

In simple terms, ghosts are the spirits left behind when people die. They can take many forms, these spirits, some invisible, some not. The one we humans seem to like most is the sort of see-through version of the person he or she or it once was. There are many other ideas as to what ghosts really are but I'll deal with those in the next chapter.

I suppose, if you're really considering the position, it would help to be well and truly dead, but, and I'm sorry if this disappoints you, even that doesn't necessarily guarantee ghostdom. Not everyone who dies gets to be one, you see. Actually, thank goodness for that . . . just imagine what it would be like if everyone who had ever lived was still floating around making a nuisance of themselves.

In this book I'll try to tell you all about the best ghosts: the scariest, the weirdest, the funniest and the nastiest.

Author's health warning: Please don't read this in a dark room all by yourself.

WHAT ARE GHOSTS?

The whole idea of dying fascinates everyone and always has. What does it actually mean? Does it just mean our money's run out and it's 'game over'? Have we simply had our go and it's time for someone else's? Do we just turn into worm food, or ashes? I'd like to think not and so would most people.

Most religions throughout the world teach of life after death. In fact the whole of Christianity is founded on belief in the resurrection of Jesus Christ and the presence of the Holy Ghost. People who follow gods, whether it be God, Allah, Brahma etc. would certainly have us believe that we've all got an immortal spirit or soul that kind of lurks around in our bodies. When our body finally pegs out, this spirit usually ends up going to an allocated place e.g. Heaven, Hell, Janna or Jahannam. However, some souls seem to stick around, refusing to clear off . . . ever, and these are the ghosts we're talking about – and in some cases, talking to . . .

There's a group of people who believe that they can contact and talk to ghosts whenever they feel like it. These chaps are called spiritualists and the ones who do the actual go-betweening are known as mediums. I'll tell you all about them later.

Whatever we believe, the idea of being able to see beyond our death is pretty groovy (even if it does scare the wits out of us at times). Throughout history, clever people like scientists, doctors and goodness knows who else, have tried to tell us what ghosts really are. So what have they found out? What are ghosts made from and why do they come back to haunt us?

Who's Who

Samuel Johnson, the famous eighteenth-century writer and clever person, was convinced that after we die, the bit that makes us *us*, and different from everyone else (apart from big noses and sticky-out ears), hangs around for a while refusing to stay in his or her coffin. Most times, according to Johnson, they just mooch about in an invisible state and we live people don't even know they're there. We only get to see the few that decide they want to be seen.

Salty Ghosts

French occult scientists right up to the twentieth century believed that when you bury someone, the salts contained in their body are released as they rot (how pleasant!). According to *les occultists*, when these salts escape, they begin to re-form in exactly the same position they were in before death. So

anything, from a person to a pig (or whatever), can appear to living mortals in more or less the same form – only made up of particles of salt. This is why you often see ghosts of people near graveyards and presumably ghosts of pigs near slaughterhouses (and why they're nearly always white).

These French scientists got so carried away with this that they even began doing experiments with blood from dead people – setting fire to it in order to see if it gave off ghostly apparitions.

German occultists, on the other hand, experimented with earth dug from graveyards and claimed they saw the spirits whizzing around in the glass retorts they used.

Unearthly Mixture

Then there are those who think that ghosts are spirits which have somehow got themselves entangled with a substance we can actually see. Spiritualists often refer to this as 'ectoplasm' which, according to those

who know, is a lightly coloured, viscous substance that actually seeps from the body of a medium (usually from the mouth). Apparently it can only usually be seen in the dark, and returns to the medium's body when all the fun's over.

Ghostly Grief

Weirder still, some spiritualists believe that ghosts are the result of terrible mental strife that has caused memories of all a person's previous actions and thoughts, as well as an almost photographic image, to be printed on what they call the Akasha or 'astral light'. It is this Akasha, allegedly, that transmits the waves of human willpower, feelings and imagination, making it possible to be interpreted by a clairvoyant. Most scientists regard this as pure bunkum.

Second Time Round

Other people reckon that we have all lived previous lives and that the ghosts we see are subconscious memories of ourselves in the clothes we once wore.

This is another form of 'reincarnation', which is the term for when dead people's souls are supposed to come back to earth in other beings (which means that next time round, you could be still you, but living in something like a hamster or jellyfish).

Most of those who accept the idea of ghosts, however, actually believe that they really are there and are not just a figment of our imagination. These spirits, they reckon, are manufactured by the dead people themselves – some better than others, of course. Otherwise we'd be tripping over the damn things everywhere we went.

GHOSTS FROM ROUND THE WORLD

All round the world, for as long as there've been people, there've been ghosts. Right back when he stopped being an ape, Early Man began to see things lurking about at the back of his cave.⋆ He and his mates buried their dead with great respect and who can blame them? They certainly didn't want visitors from the afterlife giving them a hard time. Most countries have their own ghostly history.

JUST INVENTED

⋆ *Actually there might well have been ghost monkeys as well, as you can read in the chapter on animals.*

Indian Ghosts

Some of the earliest written-about ghosts were called *Bhuts*
and go back donkey's years in Indian and Hindu mythology
– over a thousand years at least – before Jesus was born. The
correct translation of Bhut is 'has-been' which is rather
appropriate when you come to think of it. Bhuts were
believed to be the ghosts of people who died nastily or had
not been given a proper burial. There's never been such a
thing as a nice Bhut, as they have all been wicked and cruel
and no fun at all. These bad Bhuts are just the same today –
a real pain in the proverbial . . . bhut!

Hot Bhuts

Bhuts live mostly in deserts, up trees, in old abandoned
houses, around crossroads and in the roofs of ordinary Indian
people's homes. For some reason, they never – ever – touch
the ground. Bhuts usually try to scare anyone they can, bhut
– sorry – but, given the choice, prefer women, children and,
for some strange reason, newlyweds. (I'd have thought that
marriage was scary enough.)

Head Bhut!

According to Hindu mythology, the boss of the Bhuts is a
god called Shiva; a rather nasty piece of work with three
eyes, a hat made of skulls and a huge serpent dangling round
his neck. He lives high in the Himalayas with his supreme
goddess girlfriend Shakti, who's also someone you wouldn't
want to meet at a dark crossroad. I suppose their extreme
grumpiness is almost understandable, for one of their sons,
Skanda, was born with six heads and the other, Ganesha, was
given the head of an elephant. (Imagine what they must
have had to put up with at ghost school, poor dears.)

Ghost Curry

There were also believed
to be other ghosts in
India called *Bautas*.
These were horrid
little chaps with
small red bodies
and big heads with
fangs like lions.
They came out
mostly at night
and gibbered in
a high nasal
tone (remind
you of
anyone?). In
order to stay on the right side of them, the peasants would
build tall piles of stones on top of which they would leave
freshly prepared food (probably the very first takeaways).

OH NO –
NOT CURRY AGAIN

Assyrian Ghosts

Assyria was the kingdom in northern Mesopotamia that
became the centre of one of the greatest empires of the
ancient Middle East. It dates from the fourteenth to the
sixth century BC. The Assyrians believed in a rather horrid
type of ghost called an *alû* who used to terrify the natives. It
hung out in caves, ruins and abandoned buildings and was
described as 'horrible in appearance – half human and
sometimes without a mouth, ears or limbs'. Personally, I
couldn't see what harm a person with all those things
missing could do you (rub you to death?). That was until I
read that your average alû could envelop his victim like a
cloak and squeeze the living daylights out of him.

Ghost's Egyptian Style

The ancient Egyptians believed in more ghosts and demons than you could shake a mummy at. These ghosts apparently glided over the land trying to harm anyone they met. In those days Egyptians thought that man consisted of a physical body, a spiritual body, a shadow, a soul, a heart and – and this is where the trouble started – a spirit called *khu*.

Now each khu, so the story goes, felt terribly lonely when its person died and so went about causing healthy people to fall ill out of spite. It was also fond of getting right inside animals' heads and making them go crazy (good game!). Ordinary people's khus were bad enough, but the khus of people who'd killed themselves, been criminals or were unburied, were absolutely frightful and not to be meddled with at all.

Ghost Alarm

Egyptian ghosts were rather good at attacking visitors, especially those trying to nick stuff from the tombs of their ancient Pharaohs. In March 1971, Professor Walter Emery, aged 67, suffered a massive stroke in Cairo just after he'd unearthed the statue of Osiris, the Egyptian God. Unfortunately for old Walt, Osiris turned out to be the God of Death. Worse luck still, Walt had actually been searching for Imhotep, the god of medicine, who presumably could have made him better.

Leave Mummy Alone

Finding ancient mummies is a dangerous business. Over twenty-six people connected with the discovery of the tomb of Tutankhamen in 1923 came to sudden and sometimes violent ends, including Lord Carnarvon, the leader of the expedition, who'd been warned several times by mystics and seers.

WARNING!!!!

Just in case you're ever tempted to go a-mummying yourself, read this cautionary tale. Decide for yourself whether you believe it or not.

At the back end of the nineteenth century, a young man called Douglas Murray and his two chums were offered the highly ornate and priceless mummy case of a beautiful young girl, from a backstreet Arab mummy-merchant in Cairo.

PSST! WANNA BUY A CHEAP MUMMY?

Murray bought the exquisite antiquity, but a few days later was injured in a duck-shooting accident, so badly that he lost his right arm. (The duck, by the way, was fine, you'll be pleased to know.) On the journey back to England his two companions fell ill from some foreign bug and had to be dumped overboard – sorry – buried at sea. So far so bad.

Ugly Mummy

When Murray finally got home to London, he found the mummy case waiting for him. But the painted face of the pretty young girl now seemed old and real nasty. He took it to be photographed at a nearby studio, but it turned out to be the last snap the photographer ever took — he died shortly afterwards from a mystery illness (mummylaria?).

A female journalist then called round to take the mummy away and have it examined, as part of a long piece she was writing about Douglas Murray. As soon as she got the thing home, however, her mum fell down the stairs stone dead, her two champion dogs went mad (barking in fact!) and her fiancé, rather sensibly I think, ended their engagement. She, in turn, became very ill and couldn't wait to give the damn thing back to Murray. He, realising it was a bit of a liability to say the least, quickly donated it to the British Museum who were delighted.

The carrier, who was given the job of delivering the blinking thing, died a week later, as did the man employed to study the hieroglyphics on the case. The poor bloke apparently died of exhaustion having not slept a wink since he'd first clapped eyes on the mummy. But it gets worse. The press photographer, who had taken a picture of the case as it arrived at the museum, was shocked as he developed the picture. Instead of the pretty young girl he'd seen in the camera, he witnessed the face of a woman so hideous that he went into the other room and promptly blew his brains out. Now that's ugly!

The museum authorities removed the mummy from public exhibition after warders reported sobbing coming from the empty case and the museum cleaners revolted and refused to go near it. The British Museum then decided to give it to a museum in New York (which was very nice of them).

Three guesses which famous ship they sent it out on? You're right, they chose the maiden voyage of the Titanic. In 1912 the ship hit an iceberg and the mummy case sank to the bottom and was, thank God, never heard of again. Unfortunately nor were the 1500 passengers who went down with it.

Moral of the story: Never buy anything off a stranger in Cairo.

Ghosts Arab Style

If a man was murdered in an Arab country, his afrit or spectre would supposedly pop up from the ground where it had happened. The only way to get over this, so they said, was to hammer a large new nail in to the ground at the scene of the crime. This apparently pinned the poor old devil to the ground before he could get up to any mischief. This could be where the old driving-a-nail-into-a-vampire-to-kill-him idea came from. Dating afrits precisely is tricky, but they crop up in the ancient scriptures of Islam and are still believed in today.

Ghosts Abroad

Here's a weird story about a ghost who travelled all the way from the Holy Lands to England in the thirteenth century. William Longespee was brutally hacked to pieces by the fearful Arab Saracens during the Crusades. At the exact moment of his death (as it later turned out) the spectre of a knight appeared to his mother, the Abbess of Lacock, in

Wiltshire. The poor spirit looked desperately poorly and practically skeletal, so much so that even his own mum didn't recognise him. Till he spoke . . .

'I am your son William, and I have been brought down to honour God's name.' Just to prove it, he showed his mum his own personal insignia painted in ghost paint on his ghost shield. None of the Abbess's mates believed her, until six months later when official reports of her son's death, on the very same day and hour that she saw his spirit, arrived back in England.

And Now the Greeks

In ancient Greece the ghosts of good people were known as *lares* and those of the nasty ones were called *larvae* or *lemures*. The old Greeks would beat drums and burn black beans on the graves of their recent dearly departed so that the foul smell would send any lemures packing.

The Spirited Romans

Life in Ancient Rome was riddled with ghosts. You might have heard about their greatest emperor Julius Caesar (100–44BC), whose ghost came back to haunt his assassin Brutus (one of his generals). There are thousands of other Roman ghost stories. Here is one that was written down by Pliny, the famous consul.

The story goes that there was a house in Athens haunted by a male ghost who dragged a heavy ghost-chain behind him, making an awful din and frightening men, women and pets alike. Athenodouros, a famous philosopher, hired the house for a laugh to try to quieten him down. On the first night, the noisy ghost turned up as usual in the study where the philosopher was philosophising. Athenodouros thought he'd fool him by taking no notice but eventually the loud chinking noise got on his nerves. When he turned round, the ghost beckoned Athenodouros to follow him to the courtyard where it pointed to a particular spot on the ground and then vanished.

The following morning, after a good night's sleep, the philosopher took his spade and started digging at the spot. There he found the skeleton of a man bound in chains. Athenodouros then had the corpse publicly burned and the ghost was never seen again.

Chinless Chinese Ghosts

Just about every ancient Chinaman had a complete terror of ghosts – especially those of ex-murderers. They appeared, so the ancient books say, in a most peculiar way – first the head, then the feet, then the rest. The only parts that didn't appear were their chins.

The poor old Chinese did everything to try to keep on the right side of their chinless ghosts. They'd pin money and

pictures of their best warriors to the walls and perform
ceremonies like the 'Appeasing of the Burning Mouths'★
where they put plates of cakes out with invitations to the
'Honourable Homeless Ghosts'.

Hair Scare

In May 1876 complete
panic broke out in the
streets of Nanking.
Invisible demons were
tearing round
snipping off
everyone's pigtails.
For ages
afterwards, men
and women
would walk about
clutching their hair
for safety. The panic
spread to Shanghai,
but by this time the
ghosts had turned to
crushing sleeping people to
death, which was a little more serious. This hair cutting and
body crushing went on for over three years. Velly nasty
indeed.

IT WASN'T ME - HONEST

Japanese Ghosts

Old Japanese spirits, particularly from the Kamikura period
(1185–1333), were very odd: women ghosts with bad

★ *You'd have thought this would have been for those Indian curry-eating ghosts.*

haircuts wearing long white robes; legless Samurai warriors (not from drinking I hasten to add); and foxes that changed into beautiful women who'd bewitch anyone that crossed their path.

Caribbean Ghosts

If you're going to be a ghost anywhere, might I suggest the warm and sunny islands of the Caribbean? Many weird and wonderful cults came over to the Caribbean from West Africa via the slave trade in the eighteenth century. Most notable are Obeah in Jamaica and the infamous Voodoo of Haiti. Both have been connected with witchcraft and black magic but Voodoo actually mentions an ancient Supreme Being (God). These cults are, in fact, very close to spiritualism, being merely a more dramatic way of calling back, not only the spirits of their dead ancestors, but *loa*, the spirits of African gods and old Catholic saints.

The way they do it is quite simple. A group of drummers slowly builds up a rhythm while those that would like to be possessed by the spirits of the dead prance around. Usually some poor animal, like a goat or a chicken, gets its throat cut for good measure. As the pace of the drumming increases to fever pitch, the dancer goes into a sort of a trance. This is the signal for the spirit or loa to enter.

Many of the spirits are quite nice and well meaning, but apparently a *zombi* sometimes turns up which is not such good news. Zombis are supposed to be either the disembodied souls of dead people or the actual corpses themselves, which have popped up out of the ground for the party.

Most religious bodies, by the way, get their ecclesiastical knickers in a twist over this way of calling up the spirits, but, in a way, there isn't much difference between this and leaping around to gospel music, swinging incense about or falling on your knees in huge churches (just a bit more sweaty).

By the Way

If you want to keep these evil spirits away, there's a very good aerosol spray called Kitamal (Spanish for 'go away evil') for sale in South America that will, apparently, do the job nicely.

Holy Ghosts

Top of the pops of all holy ghosts was no doubt Jesus who turned into your actual 'Holy Ghost' after being crucified by the Jews. But there's another famous ghost mentioned in the Bible – in 1 Samuel 28 to be precise. The story goes like this:

King Saul was a bit worried about how his battle with the Philistines was going so he asked one of his top witches (the Witch of Endor) to call up the last king, Samuel, for some advice. A phantom duly appeared who warned Saul of certain doom. Biblical historians now believe it could well have been a trick involving clever lighting and an early version of the ventriloquist's dummy.

MODERN GHOSTS

In the olden days ghosts simply drifted around draughty old castles and stuff. These days they've got a whole lot of nice shiny machinery to play with. Here are a few examples of the tricks they can now get up to.

Happy Snaps

In 1975 a photo was published of retired RAF officer, Sir Victor Goddard's, old squadron. The snap showed a group of officers from World War I. The strange thing about it was that it included the face of air mechanic Freddie Jackson peeping over his mate's shoulder. Strange, because Freddie had been at his own funeral earlier on the very day the photo was taken – he'd been banged fatally on the head by a propeller (with the plane switched on). Silly old Sir Victor said that maybe Jackson didn't know he was dead and had turned up for the picture anyway.

Ghost Bus-ters

There have been rather a lot of fatal accidents at one particular junction in Ladbroke Grove. At the point where St Marks Road joins Cambridge Gardens, there had been reports of a strange driverless bus, with lights ablaze, running long after all the other buses were safely tucked up in their bus shelter.

Following one particularly gruesome accident, the

Paddington inquest heard from dozens of residents who'd sighted the runaway bus. Some even said they'd waited for all the tyre screeching to be over before they could get to sleep. In the end the council altered the corner and the phantom bus was never seen again. One is tempted to ask how all the other ghosts got home after that.

Ghosts on Telly

In 1993 a family in London decided to take photos of themselves while they were all together at Christmas. When the pictures came back from the chemist's there appeared to be a strange woman's face on the telly in the background. So what? I hear you say. You get lots of strange women on television on Christmas Day – there's the Queen for a start!

The trouble was – the telly had been switched off all day. When the press got hold of the strange story and published the pictures in the papers, several people commented that the woman looked just like Doris Stokes, a famous medium. Stranger still, the poor old dear had been dead for several years. Time for a new telly I'd have thought.

Ghost Rock

Here's another story from 1993. A family in Falkirk, Scotland, reported that every night at the same time their son's toy guitar played ghostly music when there was no one near it. Paranormal investigators were called in and sure enough at a given time it began to play. The guitar was duly taken away to be tested, but the damn thing refused to perform anywhere else (temperamental or what!). Weirder than that, the music continued after it was gone.

In desperation, the researchers went through a cupboard near to where the guitar had stood. Behind a whole load of household junk was a musical toy which, due to a fault, was setting itself off at the same time every night.

Ha Ha! Let that be a lesson to you. Don't believe everything people tell you.

Ghosts go Clubbing

At the end of the 1990s the alarm went off in Oldham Police station indicating a break-in at Butterflies, a local night club. The police rushed to the site and found that nothing appeared to have been disturbed. Just to make sure, they ran the security video tape. Imagine their surprise when they saw a man walking along the corridor as clear as day and then through the door at the end. Neither the manager nor his staff had ever clapped eyes on him before. Strange, but even stranger when you consider the chap hadn't opened the door first.

THE SPIRIT OF THE CITY

All cities have their ghosts, but London seems to have more than its fair share. Why not try and find these places and scare yourself witless?

Meat Off the Bone

London's Smithfield meat market goes back many centuries. In 1654 butchers began to complain about the ghost of a well-known local lawyer called Mallet who thought it great fun on a Saturday night between nine and twelve to drift between their stalls throwing all the joints of meat about (everyone to his own I suppose). Despite the angry butchers lunging at him with their knives and cleavers, they only managed to endanger each other. Pictures of him show that he wore extremely long pointy shoes by the way.

But that's not all — by far. Way back in history, Smithfield was called Smoothfield and was the site for hundreds of executions. Most famous was that of the Bishop of Rochester's cook called Roose, who was executed in 1530 for poisoning the soup of the bishop's household, killing two and causing another seventeen to be very ill.

ANY MORE FOR ANY MORE?

The method of his death was most appropriate, for he was trussed up and lowered into a huge cauldron of boiling water, which presumably made soup of him too. The poor ex-cook has also been seen (pre-cooked and ladle in hand) walking the streets of Smithfield.

During the reign of Queen Mary I, in the sixteenth century, 270 Protestants were burned to death immediately opposite the Church of St Bartholomew the Great (which is still there). In 1849, workmen excavating a sewer on the site, found a layer of ashes and human bones just three feet below the ground. In case there was any doubt as to their identity, they also dug up oak posts, together with chains and rings that the victims had been attached to. Needless to say, every now and again the occasional blood-curdling shriek and the sounds of wood burning can be heard, all accompanied by the unmistakable whiff of barbecued Protestant.

Ghost Strip

Nell Gwynne, the seventeenth-century mistress of King Charles II (1666–1685), had a reputation for being a rather 'naughty' lady, so what better place for her to haunt than a strip club? A few years ago, ladies at the famous and historic Gargoyle Club in Soho got together in the Nell Gwynne room between 'turns' and played the spooky old wineglass-in-the-centre-of-the-table game to while away the odd hour. Nothing much happened, but later when the club had closed two of the girls stayed on. The wineglass pushed out a very badly spelled version of the words NELL GWYNNE, and then began to whizz round the table. One of the girls fainted with fright and began mumbling in a strange voice. The other heard weird scraping noises coming from behind a locked door. Terrified, she yelled out of the window to some passing policemen who promptly rescued

her and her mate. Onlookers in the street saw a tall hooded figure suddenly appear on the pavement in Meard Street, but it vanished into thin air shortly after.

Over the years, other witnesses, including the famous poet (and drunk person) Dylan Thomas, claim to have seen a rather well-endowed woman wearing a flowered hat drifting across the club floor and into the lift shaft.

Riding Forbidden

Some ghosts have no regard for public bylaws. Jerry Abershaw, a famous eighteenth-century highwayman, gallops his horse at full pelt across Wimbledon Common regularly, despite signs prohibiting horse-riding between sunset and sunrise. I suppose if I'd been hanged from a gibbet on the common in 1795, I wouldn't care less about rules and regulations either.

Shot in the Dark

A woman was walking through a graveyard in Hammersmith in 1804 when a white phantom that had been seen a little earlier by some other people passing in a carriage, chased her between the gravestones. She died a little later from the shock.

Patrols of men went out for several nights to try to get to the bottom of the mystery. On the fourth night, sure enough, a figure in white was seen crossing the graveyard. Francis Smith, a customs officer, shot at the figure, but instead of the bullet passing straight through, as it should have, the figure fell to the ground. No wonder – it turned out to be painter and decorator Thomas Milwood, still in his white decorating clothes, staggering home late from the pub. Whoops!

THAT AIN'T NO GHOST

The Bloody Ghost of St James's Palace

If you really don't like ghosts then don't go near Henry VIII's Palace built in 1532 at St James's (and stop reading this book!). It is supposed to be one of the most haunted places in England. Here is just one of a hundred stories.

In the part of the Palace that looks a bit like a country house, the body of a man propped up in a bed drenched in blood has been seen many times. The story goes like this. Ernest, the Duke of Cumberland, came home one night in 1810, blind drunk after a visit to the opera followed by all sorts of rude behaviour in Covent Garden. He then, apparently, murdered his little Italian valet called Sellis by holding his hair and practically severing his head with a sword.

In court, the Duke said it was self-defence and that the little servant, who'd attacked him for no reason, had just gone to bed and slit his own throat (very likely your Lordship).

It turned out the randy old Duke had had his wicked way with the poor servant's pretty daughter, who, finding herself pregnant, committed suicide rather than face the disgrace. The Duke then did her father in to shut him up. Like all aristocracy in those days, the Duke literally got away with murder, but was booed in the streets for the rest of his miserable life.

Every now and again, even to this day, scuffling sounds can be heard in the room accompanied by the sickly smell of freshly spilt blood.

The Black Nun

Here's a sad one. For 200 years until 1973 it was our famous Guardsmen's job to patrol the vaults of the Bank of England to protect the country's gold.

But apparently they weren't the only ones walking the dingy corridors. The so-called black nun, Sarah Whitehead, still does to this day – not to protect our gold but to find her long lost brother.

Philip Whitehead, a Bank of England clerk, was arrested in 1811 and charged with forgery. He was later hanged for the crime, which sent his loving sister right round the bend. The following day she was back at the bank dressed in black from head to foot and wearing a thick veil. For over twenty-five years she walked up and down Threadneedle Street (where the bank is) asking person after person if they'd seen her poor brother.

But her death didn't end it there. Poor Sarah was buried in a graveyard that later became the Bank's formal gardens. Bank clerks at the turn of the century began to see the poor woman regularly, sobbing fit to burst and pounding her gravestone with her fists.

MORNING!

Jack's Back

Two of Jack the Ripper's most famous victims have been seen again in the city in which they were murdered. His very first victim in 1888, the prostitute Polly Nichols, was originally found with her throat slashed and her stomach cut open. Ever since, passers-by in Durward Street, Whitechapel, have spotted a stooped figure glowing eerily in the gutter.

Another of his victims, Annie Chapman, is sometimes still heard screaming in Hansbury Street, Spitalfields.

'Terry' the Ghost of Covent Garden Underground Station

Ghosts turn up in the most unlikely places with unlikely names, but none more odd than Terry the Ghost of Covent Garden Underground Station. Like most of the older underground stations, Covent Garden is a rabbit warren of dark corridors and staircases. Right up to very recently, there have been reports of a strange guy in old-fashioned clothes and pale leather gloves drifting around the station. Railway workers hate working there as they often hear strange gasps and sighs, echoey footsteps, loud banging and even the odd muted scream which, I must admit, all sounds pretty normal to me. But not, maybe, when you consider that they've all been heard well after the trains have finished running.

CAN I SEE YOUR TICKET MATE?

In the late 1950s a clairvoyant was sent to Covent Garden to see if he could sort it out. He saw the ghost almost immediately and said that it was trying to give him a name that sounded like 'Terry'. Local historians showed him a picture of William Terris, an actor-manager who'd died a long time ago in dodgy circumstances, and the clairvoyant was positive it was him.

The highly successful Terris had been stabbed in 1897 as he was leaving the Adelphi theatre (which is still there). As he was dying, he just managed to tell everyone that he'd be back – which was very nice of him. His murderer, Richard Prince, a small-time actor, riddled with jealousy, was found nearby screaming and foaming at the mouth.

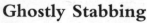

Since then, Terris has been seen all over the place – in the theatre, in the street, but most of all in the tunnels in and around Covent Garden Station.

Ghostly Stabbing

Not all ghosts are harmless. In April 1922 there was a report of a man who was happily strolling down Coventry Street, when he turned off into an alley and thought he heard footsteps behind him. He turned round but there was no one to be seen. Suddenly he felt himself being stabbed in the neck. When he was found and rushed to Charing Cross Hospital, the doctors were sure he'd been attacked by somebody even though he hadn't seen any assailant. That was until another man, and then another, turned up with exactly the same wound from exactly the same location with exactly the same story. Scary!!

The Ghost Streaker

If you like ghosts of tall old men with no clothes on, I might be able to help you (somebody should!). If you get yourself down to Cleopatra's Needle, that strange, granite obelisk by the Thames at Westminster, the shadowy figure of a man, as naked as the day he was born, can often be seen running along the wall and then diving into the river without a splash. All that is heard is a scary moaning sound and mocking laughter. I'd have thought you'd have heard the chattering of teeth too.

Ghosts at the Beeb

Everyone knows the huge BBC building in Langham Place, but few know that it's haunted. Many people claim to have seen, on the second and third floors, the ghost of an ancient butler, walking in slow motion with an empty tray. Others have witnessed, in one particular room, a large bat-like creature jumping out of a wall. And it wasn't Terry Wogan either.

The Creepy 'Tree of Death'

There's a strange tree in Green Park, I've been told, that no birds ever settle in, that no drunks ever booze under, nor lovers snog by, nor children play near. Many people have apparently hanged themselves from its gruesomely twisted branches over the years. The tall figure of a man has often been seen nearby, but is said to disappear whenever a second glance is attempted. Park attendants swear blind that sometimes when they are passing they hear strange noises, like the clashing of swords, horrible evil laughter or the odd agonised groan. This tree had been the scene of various duels and murders going right back to the eighteenth century.

I don't know about you, but I can't wait to find it.

COUNTRY GHOSTS

Despite the last chapter, I always prefer to think of ghosts living in deserted rural areas. Here are a few of the strangest ghost stories from around Britain.

The Weaver Who Wouldn't Play Dead

There's a little hamlet called Deane Combe on the edge of Dartmoor where once lived a very successful weaver called Knowles. When he died he was duly buried. But when his son arrived to take over the business the following morning, he was surprised to find his old man still there, sitting where he'd always sat, weaving away to his heart's content. The son was a bit niggled, so went to get the local parson. He, in turn, heard the weaver's shuttle from the bottom of the stairs leading to the workroom and called the spirit down. The parson reminded the ghostly Knowles, in no uncertain terms, that he was dead and had no business being there. The old dead weaver apologised but said he'd gone and died halfway through a job and had to finish it. The parson, expecting this reply, had brought a handful of earth from the graveyard and promptly threw it into the poor ghost's face. Suddenly the dead weaver turned into a large black dog. The vicar beckoned it to follow him and together they walked through a small wood to a lake below a waterfall. He then gave the dog half a walnut shell and ordered him to empty the lake with it and not rest until he had finished. To this day it is said that the dog can be seen either at midday or midnight laboriously emptying the pool one shellful at a time.

The Hairy Hands

Here's another story from Dartmoor. There's a lonely road that crosses Dartmoor between Moretonhampstead and Two Bridges. One day in June 1921, the medical officer to Dartmoor Prison was riding this road on his motorbike with his two children in the sidecar. According to the children, just as they were approaching the bridge that crosses the River Dart, the doctor suddenly yelled, 'There's something wrong, jump for it!'

The next moment the motorbike swerved and the doctor left the saddle and landed yards away . . . on his head – dead. The two children were luckily unhurt.

A month or so later, a young army officer was also motorbiking on the same stretch of road when he too was thrown from the saddle. He was only knocked out, however, and when able to speak claimed that a pair of hairy hands closed over his hands and drove him off the road.

Since then there have been several reports of old 'hairy hands' getting up to mischief. Scarier still is the fact that I found a reference in a book to the ghostly hands on that very same lonely moorland road between Two Bridges and Postbridge, going way back before cars or motorbikes were invented.

The Perils of Alcohol

There's a little pub in Norton St Philip, Somerset, called the Fleur de Lys. The building opposite it used to be the courthouse and over 300 years ago a bunch of rebels who'd supported the Duke of Monmouth were tried there. When they were found guilty, they were dragged across the road to the orchard behind the Fleur de Lys to be hanged.

One poor customer, who'd simply stopped for a beer, held the gate open for the miserable wretches as they went to their doom. The stupid soldiers accompanying them mistook him for one of the prisoners and promptly strung him up too. I always thought drinking was bad for you.

In 1974, William Harris, the current landlord, heard chains being dragged up the passage beside his pub and his wife saw a ghostly figure actually walking into the bar. (I reckon it was that bloke coming back to finish his pint.)

The previous landlord had once shut his dog in the pub office for an hour or so, only to come back and find the dog so scared out of its wits that it bolted out on to the road into the path of an oncoming car. At least the phantom drinker now has a little furry friend.

Glamis★ Castle

If you want to be guaranteed a sighting of a ghost, you could do far worse than get yourself invited to Glamis Castle, Macbeth's old place in Scotland. They've got more than ten ghosts in constant residence who are still, apparently, banging about, opening and shutting doors and making a right old nuisance of themselves. There's even a secret room which nobody can ever find.★★

Glamis Castle is supposed to have been home to the 'Monster of Glamis' who was born in 1800. This poor kid was so ugly, so they say, that they had to shut him away so that no one could see him. (So what – we did that with my brother!)

Among the other old faithfuls is the 'Grey Lady', who always hangs around the chapel; 'Earl Beardie', who lost his soul to the Devil in a card game in one of the towers and was doomed to play cards for ever (I hope he knew 'patience'); and another female, who's probably the same Lady Glamis who was burnt as a witch in Edinburgh. She always hovers above the clock tower so must be quite useful if you need to know the time. There's also a tall figure in a cloak; a bunch of characters who always stick around the Blue Room; a small woman who can sometimes be seen looking anxiously out of an upstairs window; a tongueless woman who's continually trotting (quietly) backwards and forwards across the park; 'Jack the Runner', a chap who only runs on the castle drive; a madman (with a great sense of balance) who walks across the roof on stormy nights; and a little black boy who was once a page.

★(pronounced 'glarms')
★★ I'm tempted to ask how they know it's there, but that seems a bit niggly.

With all that lot, I'm surprised there's any room for *proper* people.

Ghostly Sing-along

Castles and stately homes have always been homes for ghosts, especially if they're derelict or deserted. You've only got to see Ewloe Castle in Clwyd, Wales and you'll feel a shiver down your spine. Quite recently the present owner not only heard ghostly singing but saw a phantom shape pass straight through a hedge. His poor dog was so terrified that it went into a decline and died a couple of days later. The vet could find absolutely nothing wrong with him (apart from being dead).

Similarly, at Hardwick Hall, Derbyshire, two little girls in 1934 claimed they saw a ghost playing in the ruins. He looked real enough apparently, but the fact that he was floating around on the level where the first floor had been gave the game away. One of the girls, Winifred Chambers, remembered it vividly even when grown up. He apparently had a florid smiling face, with high buckled shoes, riding breeches, an open shirt and an apron. He was carrying a tray of drinks (a dangerous business with no floor). She took him to be an old-fashioned servant.

Monkey Business

Monks and nuns are often reported in ghostly form. Around 1977 and 1978 at Cranham, Essex, a ghostly monk appeared to motorists in St Mary's Lane, around Christmas time. Local police, always guaranteed to be somewhat sceptical, claimed it was a well-known local tramp, but unless the old boy had borrowed a monk's cowl and learned to float a few feet in the air, it couldn't have been.

Smoking Spooks

Throughout the highways and byways of Britain, phantom hitchhikers have been quite a common sight. In 1951 an American security policeman was driving around the Lakenheath Royal Air Base in Suffolk. He saw in his headlights an RAF pilot in uniform thumbing him down. He stopped to give him a lift. He had only been in the car a couple of minutes when he asked the driver for a cigarette, which he gave him. The driver then handed him his lighter and watched out of the corner of his eye as the pilot lit the cigarette. When he stopped at a checkpoint, he turned to his new companion, only to find there was no-one there, only the lighter lying on the seat – and a faint whiff of tobacco smoke.

GHOST STORIES
MOST HORRID

Quite a lot of ghost stories are rather weedy affairs. You know the sort of thing – pale ladies in long floaty dresses gliding up the stairs or drifting through graveyards. But others are really nasty.

The Curse of the Gallows

There's a tiny speck of land, called Norfolk Island in the middle of the Pacific Ocean 900 miles east of Australia. It was used as a prison by the British until the back end of the nineteenth century. There are only a few people living there now, but most of those have reported seeing the ghosts of dead convicts who were hanged there. From this grim place comes the tale of 'Barney Duffy's Curse.'

Barney Duffy was a huge Irish convict who escaped from the jail and was found by two soldiers hiding out in a hollow tree. The penalty for escaping was death by hanging. Duffy warned the soldiers – 'If you take me back to that dreadful place, you will die violently within a week of my hanging.'

They ignored his wild threat and poor old Duffy swung from the gallows as soon as he got back. End of story? Two days later the two soldiers went fishing near to where they had found the convict hiding, but the next morning their torn and mutilated bodies were found lying at the water's edge. And it wasn't fish, seagulls or mermaids that had done it.

The Bad Teacher Alert

Ever since Dame Elizabeth Hoby died in 1609, her ghost has been seen wandering around her old home, Bisham Abbey in Buckinghamshire. Poor Elizabeth, close friend of that great queen of the same name, died in misery for something she did earlier in her life.

It all started with her youngest boy William who was by all accounts a bit of a dunce at his schoolwork. In those days, before proper schools were invented, kids were often taught by their parents or governesses. Anyway William's writing-books were especially bad and although his mum would beat him with great regularity, it never seemed to do any good.

One day his spelling was worse than ever and covered in crossings-out and ink blots. His mum lost the plot completely, beating him soundly and locking him in a cupboard to teach him the lesson he'd obviously ignored. Suddenly a message came from Queen Elizabeth, saying that Dame Hoby was needed at court right away. I bet you can guess where this is going.

When she got back late that night, Dame Hoby felt sorry for her terrible temper attack earlier and went to little Will's room to apologise. He wasn't there of course. She suddenly remembered that she'd locked him in the cupboard but, when she got there, the poor kid was dead, slumped over a pile of books. In those days there was no NSPCC so Elizabeth Hoby got away with it.

Her ghost has mostly been seen drifting through the abbey grounds wringing her hands in front of her. But in 1840 workmen doing repairs found several books with children's writing in them that had slipped down beneath the floor boards under a cupboard. One of the pages was almost unreadable as it looked as if it had been drenched in tears. Let that be a lesson to all of you who don't do your homework neatly.

Horrible Hands

In my book *The Short and Bloody History of Highwaymen* I described a bizarre candle-holder that was made from the severed hand of an executed man. I thought at the time it was rather far-fetched . . . until I came across this story . . . Way back in the 1790s a woman traveller arrived at the old Spital Inn on the lonely Bowes Moor in County Durham. She asked to be allowed to sit in front of the fire for a while before continuing her journey. The landlord asked a maid to sit with her, but the maid thought it a trifle odd when she saw trousers peeping out just below the traveller's long skirts. As soon as the maid appeared to be asleep, so the story goes, the traveller brought out a dismembered hand which had a candle wedged between its fingers. It had been taken from an executed criminal. The man, for indeed the traveller was a man, then said, 'Let all who sleep, sleep on, let those who are awake be awake.' He then went to try to open the locked door to let his mates in.

The maid, who had only been pretending to be asleep, rushed upstairs to warn the landlord that the door was being broken down. He wouldn't wake up, just as the legend promised. She remembered the old tale that said that this particular type of candle (which was still burning on the table downstairs) could only be put out with milk. The maid dashed to the kitchen and tipped a whole jug over the hand.

The landlord and his staff woke instantly and heard the commotion downstairs. The robbers left with nothing apart from a load of shotgun pellets in their backsides.

By the way, the candle holder was known as the 'Hand of Glory' and the actual candle had to be made from fat from the hanged man's flesh, virgin wax and something called Lapland sesame oil, should you want to make one.

The Bell Witch

In the eighteenth century in Tennessee, John Bell, a rich plantation owner and chum of President General Andrew Jackson, was plagued by a jolly unpleasant ghost in his huge plantation house. He called in an investigator called William Porter, who agreed to sleep over.

On the very first night Porter had the rather alarming experience of having a ghost jump into his bed, roll up the bedclothes into a tight ball and give off the foulest smell imaginable. Porter was, as you can imagine, rather put out (he could probably have thought of better things to jump into his bed). He grabbed the ball of smelly bedclothes with the idea of chucking them out but found them so heavy that he couldn't even lift them. Eventually the stink was so bad that he had to rush out into the cold night air to get away from it.

Worse Still

Following this, between the years of 1771 and 1821, one of the children in the Bell household began puking up pins and needles, which is all right if you have a load of sewing to do, but otherwise . . .

John Bell died mysteriously in 1821 from poisoning and soon after a huge glowing ball came out of his chimney, blew apart and a loud voice was heard to say, 'I'm going to be gone for seven years.' Everyone presumed it was the ghost and was naturally rather pleased. Nobody seems to know if the ghost kept his word.

INANIMATE GHOSTS

Most people think ghosts are only see-through versions of dead people. Throughout history, however, all sorts of things have come back to haunt us.

Home is Where the Head is

Bits of the body are always good in haunting circles, but none better than the human skull. Theophilus Brome's is a good example. Theophilus was a Royalist soldier during the English Civil War in the seventeenth century, who went over to the Roundheads because he couldn't bear what his side was doing to their prisoners – chopping their heads off, shoving them on spikes and waving them around as trophies. When, in 1670, he was old and about to die, he asked his sister if it wasn't too much trouble to have his head taken from his body so no-one could do the same to him. He asked, also, that it should never leave the house that he had lived in all his life.

Since that time, many of the tenants of that particular farm in Yeovil, Somerset, have attempted to get rid of the dratted thing only to be scared silly by the sound of horrid screaming. One was so upset that he decided to put the skull back in the grave with the rest of Theophilus. When the spade snapped in half while digging up the grave, it seemed pretty clear

I DID WARN YOU

that this might not be the best idea in the world, so they stopped and took the skull home again. It still lives happily in Higher Chilton Farm and has actually brought good luck to many of the subsequent inhabitants.

Having said that, on one occasion in the 1970s, Dave Allen, the Irish comedian, visited the farm to do a programme. He was apparently so scared by something that happened on the way home that he swore he'd never go near the place again, friendly skull or no friendly skull.

Spooky Bristol

For some obscure reason, the city of Bristol can often be seen floating in the sky over Alaska between 21st June and 10th July. Why Bristol? Nobody knows. It was first reported by the indigenous Alaskans way before the first white settlers arrived, although I reckon they wouldn't have known what a city (let alone Bristol) was. In 1887 a famous pioneer, William Willoughby, was so gobsmacked by the apparition that he decided to take its photo (which I've actually seen). Despite his protestations, hardly anyone could believe that it wasn't just a picture of – er – Bristol. Since then, many ghost cities have been seen in the Alaskan skies, but most of them are said to look like ancient cities from the past. I bet you think I'm making this up.

Ghost Ships

The Chief of the Campbell Clan, the Duke of Argyll, still has the picture of a strange galley, complete with sails and oars, on his coat of arms. Legend has it that when any prominent member of the family dies, the ship appears on Lock Fyne at Inveraray in Scotland.

The ship was seen by hundreds of people in 1913, at the death of Lord Archibald Campbell, sailing across the loch with its usual crew of three seamen. It was observed to take its usual course and then, when it reached the shore, it continued overland to the sanctuary of St Colomba.

The Flying Dutchman

A nineteenth-century Dutch captain called Hendrik van der Decken attempted to sail his ship in a terrible storm round the Cape of Good Hope, despite the pleading of his crew. The ship went down like a stone, but legend has it that the silly captain, who had listened to the Devil rather than God, was condemned to sail the seas for all of eternity in his ghostly ship while luring other ships to the same fate. The legend also goes on to say that the now ghostly captain eventually said he was sorry for what he had done, but by then his crew were deaf skeletons and would have none of it.

The most convincing sighting was in 1939 when over a hundred people saw the ship, in full sail, passing Glencairn Beach in False Bay, near Cape Town. There was not a breath of wind that day.

The most famous witness was Prince George, who later became George V (1910-1935). He and many others saw the vessel on the night of 11th July 1881 off the southern coast of Australia. He said it gave off an eerie light which lit up all its masts and sails. Although the officer of the watch and the quarterdeck midshipman also saw her, when they all dashed up to the front of the boat to get a better view, she'd disappeared without trace. It was a clear, calm night.

I don't want to pour cold water on their story, but I recently read that there's an atmospheric condition called 'St Elmo's Fire' which causes the ends of masts and spas on sailing ships to glow with an eerie, greenish light.

Now You See it, Now You Don't

In the 1930s, a young girl called Edna Hodges was cycling along an old Roman road called Ermine Street (just outside Swindon) to visit her friend. A storm blew up and it started to rain. The little girl, frightened of the thunder, decided to ask for shelter at an isolated little thatched cottage that looked warm and welcoming. She was met at the door by a tall man with a grey beard and

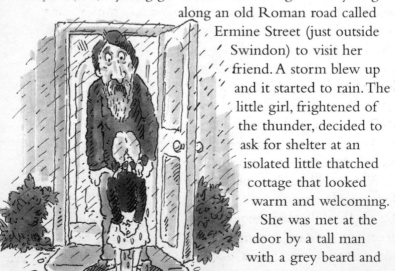

he beckoned her to come in. Oddly enough, when she got inside the cosy cottage all sounds of the raging storm disappeared. The old man smiled but never spoke (he sounds a darn sight more dangerous than the storm). Suddenly, young Edna found herself back on the road on her bike, continuing on her journey, having no memory of actually leaving the cottage.

When she turned up at her friend's house, the girl's parents, who'd been worried about her getting soaked, were all mystified as she was perfectly dry. She explained what had happened but was told that the only house along that stretch of road was completely derelict and hadn't been occupied for years and years. I think I'd rather have got wet – how's about you?

The Blank Cheque

On 28th November, 1931, a Miss Ina Jephson received a letter from her solicitor containing a cheque for ten pounds (quite a lot in those days). She couldn't get to the bank that day, so carried the cheque around in her bag, looking at it occasionally to make sure it was still there. She remembered clearly that the paper had a blue marbled pattern. When she got home, she looked again, but this time it was gone. She searched high and low for the thing, but in the end had to write to the solicitor to tell him she'd lost it and ask him to stop the payment.

How could he? he replied in the following letter, he hadn't sent it yet. He enclosed the real cheque which, according to Miss Jephson, was identical to the first 'ghost' one.

57

The Plane Truth

Sir Michael Bruce, a former airforce pilot, was once sent on
an instruction course to Larkhill in 1944 with other flyers.
Part of their instruction involved finding suitable sites for
gun emplacements. Five senior officers and the young Bruce
went off in a jeep to mark one of these sites.

They were travelling along the road that passes
Stonehenge when they all saw a small aircraft that appeared
to be in trouble. They watched it fly lower and lower and
then dive headlong into a clump of trees. The men raced to
see if they could save the pilot, but found nothing when
they got there. Suddenly one of them called the others over
to a stone cairn. His face was ghostly white as he read that it
had been built as a memorial to the very first death from a
plane crash in England in 1912. Phew!

ANIMAL GHOSTS

If your dog, cat or even bunny rabbit dies, fear not, you might well see them again. Animals make good ghosts as the next few examples will suggest.

The Ghost Bear of Cheyne Walk

There's a house in Cheyne Walk, in the most fashionable bit of Chelsea, that was supposed to have been built on the site of an old bear-baiting ring. Tormenting bears was all the rage in the seventeenth century. All over London there were special arenas where the poor things were blinded and then torn to pieces by specially bred mastiffs – for fun! A particular phantom bear has been seen by several occupants stumbling around the garden in a frenzy (that's the bear, not the occupants).

Mind you, that's nothing – another person of the same house was known to rush from the living room every time she saw the vision of a woman lying on the sofa with her throat cut. The house had been the scene of a particularly horrid murder long ago.

Beware – Frozen Chicken Alert!

Be warned. If for any reason you venture anywhere near Pond Square in Highgate, you might be in for a big surprise. A frightful phantom chicken has been seen many times, as naked as the day it came out of its egg, shivering, squawking at the top of its beak and running round in ever decreasing circles. It actually happens to be one of the most famous hens in history.

In 1626, the famous Francis Bacon – politician, writer and scientist – had been travelling home in his coach one snowy winter's day when he noticed that the snow removed by the carriage wheels revealed fresh green grass despite its having been covered for weeks (strange bloke!). Aha! – he thought – if snow can preserve grass, perhaps it can preserve other things. So saying, he ordered his coachman to go and buy a chicken from the farm up the road (as you would) then throttle it, pluck it and fill the poor clucker with snow. He then got him to put the hapless hen in a bag and stuffed more snow round it.

It was, as we now know, the very first frozen chicken. Unfortunately Sir Francis wasn't around to witness his momentous discovery. The silly chap caught a cold while the experiment was being carried out and died of pneumonia only a couple of days later.

Oddly enough, Sir Francis Bacon himself has never been seen in ghostly form ... but that darned chicken has! She's been seen over twenty times in the twentieth century alone. The last sighting was in 1970 when a couple, who were canoodling on a doorstep in Pond Square, were surprised when a big, white, naked bird dropped to the ground in front of them (some people have all the luck). It was the chicken, in case you're wondering – and after flapping about for a few seconds, it disappeared into thin air.

Hellhounds

The most common four-legged phantoms are usually known as hellhounds and take the form of huge black dogs. Most deserted regions have them and some people believe that the mad donkey mentioned in the next bit is really just a massive three-legged version.

The most popular (if you can use that word) hellhound is called 'The Black Shuck' and he prowls around the lonely fenlands of East Anglia, finding his way around by the light from his huge, single red eye.

During World War II, a young American airman and his wife were renting a small hut on the edge of the Walberswick Marshes near to the air base where he served. One fearful night, there was a dreadful pounding on the door. Looking through the window, the young man saw it was the dreaded Black Shuck. He'd only heard about it a few days before and was scared out of his wits. The terrified couple piled what furniture they had against the door while the hellish hound bit and scratched in a frenzy from the outside. Rather like the big bad wolf in the story of the three little pigs, Black Shuck tried everything to get in and even jumped on to the flat roof, tearing at it with his huge teeth.

Several hours later the poor couple's torment ended and they ventured outside. They naturally expected to find the wooden hut covered in scratch and bite marks, but there was no sign of any attack – not even a single paw mark in the damp soil surrounding their home. They moved shortly afterwards.

The Shaggy Donkey Story

Around the city of Leeds there have been reports of a dreadful shaggy donkey with huge eyes like red saucers. The natives call the beast 'Padfoot' and swear that it only runs on three legs. To see it is not very good, as it's supposed to indicate death not far round the corner.

Bull, Book and Candle

The wall of Hyssington Church, Bagbury, has a huge crack from top to bottom. It was caused by a ghastly phantom bull who was supposed to be the ghost of an evil parishioner – name unknown (Mr Bull?). Apparently this bull terrorised the neighbourhood, eventually causing a posse of twelve local parsons to chase it round the churchyard with bell, book and candle (a traditional method of excluding people from all things religious). The bull apparently disappeared as it charged into the wall and was never seen again.

The Ghostly Pigeon

I've never liked pigeons much – nasty flappy things that poo everywhere. Flying rats I calls 'em. There was once a famous Australian opera singer, however, called Dame Nellie Melba (1861-1931), who became well-known for her pet white pigeon (and a dessert called peach melba).

Except it wasn't really! The bird was no more than a ghost and nobody else ever saw it. The ghost that followed her everywhere, supposedly bringing her good luck. It became so much a part of her life that, in the end, she wouldn't go on stage unless she could actually see it fluttering about.

Monkey Business

There was a Polish medium called Franck Kluski who

produced some weird apparitions at his seances. Between 1913 and 1923 he became famous for producing animals and birds and nobody has ever been able to explain how he did it (or why, come to that). He even arranged for photographs to be taken to prove their existence.

The first was a huge hawk-like bird that scared the wits out of the other sitters by flying round the room bashing everything and everyone with its wings, before settling on old Kluski's shoulders. Next was a small, weasely thing which scampered across the table and sniffed the hands and faces of the astonished sitters with its cold little nose. Just as they were recovering, Kluski produced a huge black dog with massive fangs and glowing eyes, usually accompanied by an old man who stopped it from biting everyone.

But all of this was nothing compared to his final offering, which took the form of a huge shaggy half ape, half human which, though relatively friendly, would think it a great laugh to lift up the sofas and bookcases over his head, and even the heaviest members of the audience – in their chairs. He was last seen in 1922.

Other mediums have produced seals, cats and one even managed a phantom pig.

Ghost Pork

Talking of pigs, there is a rather odd story of a haunting by a whole herd of porkers who lived in the Chiltern Hills. A farmer, called Mr Brown, when a lad, lived in a small house called Moat Grange. The house stood at the crossing of four roads which was a traditional site for hanging criminals. One night the Brown family (that's Mr Brown, Mrs Brown and all the little Brownies) was woken by the most terrible commotion. Looking over at the crossroads they saw a whole load of spooky spotty things that looked like pigs, fighting and tearing up the ground where all the bad people had been buried. The horrified family then had to witness a horrible white face that pressed itself against the window and stared at them.

The ghostly porksters eventually stopped what they were doing and rushed off down the road into the darkness. Shortly after, the Brown family left the farm realising it was haunted. The pigs were thought at first to be the ghosts of the executed criminals. Later ghost-hunters reckon they were probably just the ghosts of ordinary pigs who felt some sympathy with the ex-criminals.

OINK

Here Pussy!

Cats have always been associated with witches and spells –
especially black ones. Before we get into ghost cats let me
tell you of some of the silly superstitions connected with
them.

1   If a cat is seen washing its face, expect rain.

2   If ever a cat is seen frolicking on the deck of a ship, it's
time to batten down the hatches, as a storm is probably
on its way.

3   If an ember jumps from the fire onto your cat, expect an
earthquake immediately.

4   In Normandy, France, it is still believed that if you see a
tortoiseshell cat climbing a tree, you can confidently
expect to be killed in an accident.

5   If a black cat crosses your path in the moonlight, you'll
probably suffer a grim death from an epidemic.

6   If two black cats cross your path between 4 and 7 a.m.
you can expect to be dead before the day's out.

7   If a strange white cat mews on your doorstep, you must
prepare to get married.

(I don't know which is worse 6 or 7. Answers on a
postcard.)

Cats were also used as cures in ancient times. French
sorcerers were rather fond of sprinkling the blood drawn
from the vein located under a poor moggie's tail to cure
skin complaints (how embarrassing). If you were blind,
they'd blow the ashes of a roasted cat's head (black) into
your eyes three times a day. Which brings us back to ghosts.
The natives of the Hebrides (a group of little islands off the
west coast of Scotland), right up to 1750, believed that cats
had amazing occult properties. Best of all was 'second sight',
the ability to see beyond what us mere mortals see. (You

often get that feeling when you see a cat staring wide-eyed into an empty space). To get yourself in touch with the workings of a cat's mind, they reckoned you had to sacrifice as many black cats as you could get your mitts on. This is how they did it (cat lovers, please leave now).

First they fastened a black cat to a spit and roasted it slowly over a low fire. As soon as the poor puss was done, they cooked another, and then another without stopping. Eventually the poor cats' caterwauling became so continuous and loud that it summoned up a horde of ghost cats who joined in the chorus. When the noise reached pandemonium level, a massive spectral cat would suddenly appear. This cat, who apparently spoke perfect English (or Scottish), promised the guy doing all the roasting any wish . . . provided he stopped what he was doing. Nine times out of ten, the cat roaster would ask for the gift of second sight which was highly sought after in the Hebrides (and a bunch of new cats I'd have thought?).

The Cat and the Baboon

Now here's a weird one to finish.

In 1840 a Mr Bishop bought a house called 'Swallows' on a two-acre plot just close to a small village near Basingstoke. He'd only been there a fortnight when two of his servants resigned claiming that the place was haunted by a large cat and a baboon – a trifle odd I'd have thought. If that wasn't bad enough, they swore they heard screams coming from the attic near where they slept, and the groans of people being strangled and tortured from the cellar under the dairy. The news spread through the village like wildfire and people came from far and wide to see for themselves. Several villagers claimed to have seen the cat and the baboon coming from the grating of the dairy cellar.

By this time old Mr Bishop had had enough, and decided to get rid of the house. He managed somehow to sell it to a mad old colonel in 1842, but the poor old buffer lasted even less time. Trying to sell a house with resident ghosts is practically impossible, so it was pulled down to make room for a row of cottages. The trouble with ghosts is that once in they refuse to move, and these were no exception. Nobody would live in these cottages so they were pulled down shortly after they were built, forming the first haunted allotments.

So who and what were these ghosts? The most popular story is that 'Swallows' was occupied by a famous highwayman called Steeplechase Jock (his dad was a Scottish chieftain) who plied his trade in the area and buried his victims around the premises. He was said to have had rather an unpleasant end – turning completely mad and throwing himself into a vat of boiling tar. The ape and the cat were supposed to be the ghosts of poor Jock and his horse, though heaven knows why (or which was which).

NICE TO SEE YOU – AGAIN

Ever since time began people have tried their level best to get in touch with their ex-nearest and dearest. The quickest and safest way is through a movement called 'spiritualism'.

Born in New York

In 1847, in the small American town of Hydesville, the Fox family heard rapping all night (and it wasn't from next door's stereo). Mrs Fox apparently asked the noise if it was a spirit and if so to knock twice. Two ear-splitting bangs followed. Mrs Fox then communicated with the 'spirit' through a series of raps until she found out (heaven knows how) that the knocker was the ghost of a pedlar who'd been murdered by the last tenant and buried in the basement. The person in question denied it emphatically, but over fifty years later, a false wall was discovered and behind it a pile of human bones.

This didn't help the poor Fox family. By that time, the raps had turned into bloodcurdling groans and there were sounds that were remarkably like a body being dragged across the floor. It all caused poor Ma Fox's hair to turn white. Eventually the spirit let it be known that 'the truth' must be proclaimed to the world and, from nowhere, hundreds of newfangled mediums found out that they could talk to the spirits. This all culminated in the birth of the spiritualist movement which was launched in the Corinthian Hall, New York, in 1849 and within a couple of years had swept across the Christian world.

Mediums Not Rare

Nowadays spiritualist mediums are everywhere – there's probably one within a few streets of where you live. These rather odd people claim to be able to get in touch with the spirits of the dead and even make a living from it. If you suddenly want to have a word with your ex-Great Auntie Nellie, for instance, you could do worse than trot round to your local medium and ask him to call her up for you. Usually there'll be a few other people at this 'seance' all wanting a brief word with their dear departed.

The idea is that you all sit in a circle holding hands in the dark while the medium goes into a sort of a trance. Then he or she asks if there's anyone out there. Well, not just anybody, only spirits connected in some way with those in the room. Suddenly, if you're lucky, you hear your Great Auntie Nellie speaking through the medium and you can talk to her. Just imagine: –

'Hello, Auntie Nellie, are you having a nice time in heaven?'

'I would be if you lot wouldn't keep disturbing me, why can't you leave me in peace?'

'Sorry, you miserable old bag, I thought you might not be quite so grumpy up there.'

This is how seances usually go, but loads of these mediums have been found to have quite elaborate tricks up their sleeves to fool people like you and me. Tape-recorders behind curtains, people moaning from other

rooms or even the weird white stuff that appears to come from their mouths called ectoplasm, which I've mentioned before. This stuff is supposed to be a substance halfway between the spirit world and the one we live in.

Do-it-Yourself Seances

I mentioned in 'London Ghosts' the strippers who sat round of an evening trying to summon up dead spirits. There used to be another sort of game that you could actually buy in Victorian shops called *Ouija* (from the French and Germans words for 'yes').

This sort of thing was all the rage in the pre-telly late-nineteenth century, either as a fun game for all the family or to be used in a seance. The Ouija board was an oblong piece of wood with all the letters of the alphabet written round its edge in a half moon shape. On top of this a much smaller, heart-shaped board mounted on tiny castors was placed. Each person would then put their index finger on the heart-shaped board and it would move around spelling out answers to questions. Unfortunately many people didn't really know what they were getting into, and there were horrendous stories of the 'players' being scared out of their wits. Certainly not to be tried at home.

Painting By Memory

Have you ever seen the paintings of L. S. Lowry (1887-1976)? He's the bloke who was a rent collector by day and in the evenings did all those little matchstick men running about the streets of the industrial town of Salford – oop north somewhere. Another painter called William Turner managed to get the famous old man to sit for the one and only oil painting ever to be done of him. Unfortunately, Turner was a bit on the slow side, so much so that poor old Lowry died mid-painting, and Turner had to finish it from memory.

Just as he was about to flog the painting in 1993, a well-known medium claimed he'd been visited by the now very dead Lowry. While chatting, the old ghost had mentioned not only that he was still doing a few drawings, but also that he quite liked the painting that Turner had done of him. He then went on to say that the work should be sold in aid of a local charity (run by the medium no doubt). Poor old Turner had to abide by his wishes.

Loads of famous people are supposed to come back through mediums, including John Lennon, Marilyn Monroe and George Orwell. Even the infamous cowperson Jesse James turned up saying he hadn't really meant to shoot all those people. Who would you like to talk to if you could bring them back? I'd like to give that Mr Hitler a piece of my mind.

SORRY FOLKS

GHOST HORSE

Poltergeists

Poltergeists are sort of ghosts that you can't actually see, and the word 'poltergeist' comes from Germany and means 'noisy spirit'. Poltergeists have a bad reputation but not all poltergeists are nasty, and some even seem to have a sense of humour. Although many become infamous for chucking furniture around and generally making a fearful mess, there

are reports of some that have actually been known to break in simply to tidy things up. We could all do with one of them.

If one of the main differences between poltergeists and ghosts is that the former can't be seen, the other is that they tend not to hang around one place for very long – sometimes disappearing in a matter of weeks. Others get attached to a particular person rather than a place, and follow him or her around.

Poltergeists have hardly ever done anyone any physical harm, tending to act more like naughty schoolboys, simply out for a laugh. Just how much of a laugh you'll find out from the following reports.

Pandemonium at Number 50

The address was the very posh Berkeley Square in London and the year was 1840. Although number 50 was empty of furniture, neighbours began to hear the sounds of massive articles being dragged across the upstairs floors. Also the bells used for summoning servants would resound throughout the deserted house in the middle of the night. When investigators entered, all they found were the bells swinging – but no further sound was heard.

Worse was still to come. At the peak of the activity, several windows were flung open by invisible hands, and stones, books and even old shoes were flung into the street below. Finally, one morning, passers-by noticed that every window in the house had been smashed.

Why this house in particular? The story goes that long before this all happened, a mad member of a very aristocratic family was held in one of the rooms and fed through a slit in the door owing to his extreme violence. After he died there were several reports of a pulsating mass of evil-smelling, panting matter with dozens of little red eyes, that would spread throughout that haunted room. Who hasn't got one of them?

Well, when a young man-about-town, Sir Robert Warboys, heard about the strange goings-on at Number 50 he accepted a challenge to sleep there overnight. He didn't believe a word of the stories but was made to take a gun with him just in case. His pals also insisted that they stand guard downstairs from the dreaded room where Sir Robert was to stay. Poor Robert had only been in the room for forty-five minutes when they heard a single gunshot. When they reached the room they found their friend slumped across the bed – dead. But he hadn't been shot. His expression told all – eyes wide open and lips curled hideously over his clenched teeth. He had simply died of fright.

The house stood empty for years (are you surprised?) but on Christmas Eve 1887, two slightly inebriated sailors, knowing nothing of its reputation and having just docked in London, broke in for somewhere to stay for the night. They woke up to a shapeless mass moving around the house. Terrified, one of them, Robert Martin, managed to flee the house to get help. When he returned with a policeman, they found his friend Edward Blundell on the ground with his face in the most horrible grimace. His neck had been snapped like a twig.

If you are completely bonkers and want to visit the house, it's still there, and the last I heard of it – it was a bookshop.

The Painting Poltergeist.

Matthew Manning achieved fame at the tender age of fifteen when he became a psychic. Unfortunately it all went a bit pear-shaped when in 1970 a poltergeist decided to concentrate on his family's 200-year-old house. This particular poltergeist became famous throughout the world

for his crazy stunts like bending cutlery and painting frenzied pictures in the style of famous old masters. Why complain? You could probably make quite a bit of dosh, I'd have thought.

Manning, by the way, turned from stylish party tricks to spiritual healing at which he became even more famous.

Hair Today Gone Tomorrow

I described in an earlier chapter how Chinese ghosts cut off the pigtails of the people in the streets of Nanking. This hair removal lark seems to be all the rage with poltergeists. In 1837, at Menomonie, Wisconsin, a poor little girl was standing with her mother when out of the blue, huge chunks of her hair simply disappeared into thin air leaving her practically bald. In another instance, in 1969, one of Bishop James Pike's assistants awoke to find her hair singed off in a straight line. This happened again and again until three weeks later when some of the locks appeared on her pillow beside her. The bishop put it down to his son's recent suicide. Perhaps he'd been a closet hairdresser.

Better the Devil You Know

Here's a bizarre one. In 1889, a farmer named George Dagg, who lived in Quebec province, Canada, noticed weird things happening around the milking parlour. Milk pans were overturned, windows smashed and small fires began to crop up everywhere. The 'focus' for all this stuff was a small orphan girl named Dinah McLean, who was often found screaming after the poltergeist had attacked her. At first she was the only person who could hear it, but later it muttered very rude things indeed to George Dagg, in a low, gruff voice, and then claimed it was the Devil.

I BEG YOUR PARDON

BARKING!

It finally agreed to leave and, on the day in question, hordes of villagers turned up to hear it, through George, supplying all sorts of personal and somewhat embarrassing information about them. Then it claimed it wasn't a Devil after all, but an angel sent by God (a very odd foul-mouthed angel at that). The following day some village children swore they'd watched a 'beautiful man in white' rising into the sky.

THINGS THAT GO BUMP IN THE NIGHT

Many things that happen can't necessarily be explained by the term ghosts. We've all heard bumpings and creakings in the night and have all seen scary faces in everyday objects when we're not even trying. Here are a few of the oddest things.

Light Fantastic

Some of the most common sightings are lights which either fly through the air, whiz across a room, or just hover in the sky. These can be interpreted as fairies, UFOs, will-o'-the-wisps or whatever, but there's usually a perfectly good explanation.

Some scientists have described a commonly seen phenomenon as 'floating ball' lightning and claim it's perfectly harmless, but an inquisitive child was reported in 1943 to have kicked out at one and the resulting explosion killed him and eleven unfortunate cows who happened to be standing nearby.

In Wales they call these floating lights 'corpse candles' and they are said to predict imminent death. On one occasion, a whole coach-load of passengers on the way from Llandilo to

Camarthen spotted three pale lights hovering over a river. The next day three men were drowned when their coracle capsized at exactly the same spot.

Old Red Eye

In 1965 a moving light chased and caught a chap called Terry Pell who was driving his vegetable lorry towards Warminster in Wiltshire. The light was like a huge red eye and stuck itself to his windscreen. Mr Pell's wife and daughter, who'd been asleep at his side, woke up and were terrified at the apparition. It then detached itself and soared off into the distance.

Forty-five minutes earlier, Mrs Rachel Atwill, who lived a few miles away, noticed a bright light in the sky accompanied by a horrible droning noise that lasted twenty-five minutes. It gave poor Mrs Atwill a headache and she was forced to have a large brandy to calm herself down. (Maybe she had the large brandy before seeing the light and hearing the noise.)

Glow Toe

If you think that's spooky, what about the American woman who noticed, just as she was going to bed, that the fourth toe on her right foot was glowing. When she rubbed it, the light spread up her foot and began to smell nasty. Her husband told her to wash her foot (I'm not surprised) but it had no effect. The light eventually disappeared after about forty-five minutes, never to return.

Beware the Invisibles

In some places ghosts are called 'invisibles'. These are particularly nasty as you will realise from the following two stories. In 1761, near Ventimiglia in Northern Italy, five peasant women were returning from the woods where they'd been collecting sticks for the fire. Without any warning, one of them screamed out and fell to the ground as cold as yesterday's pasta.

When her friends came near they were sickened by what they saw. Her clothes were finely shredded and thrown all around her up to six feet away. A huge wound on her head exposed her skull, and her stomach had been ripped open exposing her intestines. If that wasn't bad enough, most of the flesh from one thigh had been removed and her femur pulled from its socket. Doctors examining the body found no sign of blood and reckoned that she looked just like the victim of an explosion.

Poor Little Harry

One poor boy had obviously upset one of these invisibles. In 1850, a Dr Phelps's young son, Harry, became the victim of a terrible series of attacks. As he walked down the street stones were thrown at him from nowhere, and at home he would sometimes be lifted so high from his chair that his head would bang on the ceiling. Imagine that when you're having your tea!

WILL YOU PLEASE SIT PROPERLY

Once, in front of a large group of people, he was lifted right up into a tree and his clothes were shredded before the poor lad was tossed into a water tank.

Poor Little Eleonore

Lastly – and if you're still not convinced – in a pamphlet written in 1850 there was a description of a series of attacks on children. One little girl, called Eleonore Zugum, was seen to be throttled by an invisible hand which pressed in the sides of her neck. Later on, other children were pulled about and even spat on. Witnesses then watched in horror as the children were bitten more than twenty times on their arms leaving tooth marks and rings of foul-smelling spit in the shape of mouths.

VAMPIRES

Lots of people don't believe in ghosts – but they do believe in vampires. Vampires are dead people who leave their graves at night to suck the blood of the living – for a living. Here are a few for you to mull over.

Peter Plogojowich

This well-known vampire apparently lived in the village of Kisilova in Hungary in the eighteenth century. After terrorising the poor villagers for six weeks after his death, they opened his grave and found him still dead but actually looking better than ever. His skin was pink and his nails and hair had grown. His mouth, however, was full of fresh blood from his victims, which rather gave the game away. The villagers then whipped old Peter out of the coffin and burned him to a cinder, which seemed to do the trick nicely.

Strangers in the Night

This strange story comes from a tribunal in Belgrade, Yugoslavia. Government officials, along with a doctor, travelled to a certain village following the tale of a soldier who'd been invited to dinner by a pleasant peasant and his family. While eating, so the story goes, a complete stranger came into the room and joined them (odd!). Everyone seemed frightened apart from the soldier, but he kept quiet out of politeness. The next day the peasant was dead, and a couple of the others spoke up and said that the mysterious guest had been his grandfather who'd passed away over ten years before. The old boy had been suspected of being a vampire for ages. When they investigated the old stiff's tomb, he too was in perfect nick, and when they opened a vein, fresh blood squirted out. (I hope you're not having your tea while reading this.) Anyway, they chopped off the old bloke's head, hoping that would do it, but at that point several people came forward and claimed that he'd been a member of a sort of local vampire club. They then opened

four more graves only to find the inhabitants also looking absolutely marvellous (for dead people!). They were all nailed into their coffins and burned.

Arnold Paul of Madreiga

Arnold Paul lived on the Turkish–Serbian border in the eighteenth century. He was well known in his village because he was always moaning about being pestered by an old Turkish vampire, and who could blame him for that? Poor Arnold was killed one day when a hay cart toppled and fell on him. Luckily he'd managed to dine on some earth from the said vampire's grave before he died, which apparently was a well-known way to keep the inhabitant quiet.

Unfortunately it didn't work and old Arnold turned into a bigger and better (or worser) vampire than the Turk had ever been. When in 1730 they opened his coffin he was covered in blood which was bubbling from out of his veins. The local bailiff ordered that his heart be pierced, but when it was done, Arnold screamed at the top of his voice. Some people never learn.

Vampire Calling

Here's a good one. A vampire from a village called Blow, in Bohemia, used to call his victims to him and then have his bloody way with them. Eventually the villagers got wise to this and, opening his grave, tied him to a post stuck firmly in the earth.

'How friendly you are,' the corpse said in a deep voice, 'to give me a stick with which I can drive away the dogs.' Nice to find a vampire with a sense of humour, I think.

Anyway, they'd hardly left before he'd risen again and suffocated five people. The next day, the local hangman dug him up and, using a metal spike, filled him with holes. They then carried him to a huge fire, but as they walked, he howled at the top of his voice and thrashed his arms and legs.

Vampire Viewing

Do you want to see a real live vampire? (Or should that be a real dead vampire?) You can, so I'm told, if you dare hang around probably the spookiest and fabulousest graveyard in England at night. Highgate Cemetery in North London, has 45,000 graves and the whole place reeks of ruin and decay with overgrown catacombs and vaults everywhere you look. It's a dead cert for ghosts and vampires. All this, and it's open to the public – brilliant stuff!

There are reports galore of ghostly goings-on, none more scary than the one about a terrifying old woman, with long white hair, who glides amongst the scary tombs and in and out of the mouldering vaults. She's thought to be the ghost of a mad woman who in younger life murdered her own two kids, before starting on a long career as a vampire. She now tours the vast cemetery forever searching for the graves of those whose blood she'd sucked. Something to do of an evening, I suppose.

Getting Rid of Unwanted Vampires

Vampires, as you can imagine, can be a bit of a nuisance. If you are currently troubled by them, there's a simple kit you can put together to keep the nasty things at bay. Firstly, you'll need to know if the person you suspect is one *is* one. This is quite simple. Take a normal hand mirror and hold it up to him or her. If you can't see their reflection then you could be in trouble.

To keep him or her at bay, you could wear a string of garlic round your neck (it'll probably keep everyone else at bay too) – or wave a silver cross at them. (If you suspect they might be werewolves, shoot 'em with a silver bullet.) Failing that, and if you know which grave they live in, you could do far worse than the old stake-through-the-heart routine, which is practically guaranteed to finish 'em off.

WHERE'VE I GONE?

GHOST HUNTING AND WHAT TO DO IF YOU SEE ONE

Going out specially to look for ghosts is pretty pointless. Just like buses, they're never there when you want them – unless they're ghost buses (see page 27).

More Than Meets the Eye

People still try to find ghosts, however, and every year some new gizmo or other is brought out to try and fool ghosts into revealing themselves. Forget tape recorders and thermometers, they're very old hat. Nowadays your average ghostbuster uses quite elaborate see-in-the-dark video cameras, which they let run all night (while they're down the pub no doubt). One of these is called 'The Spider' and was developed by a famous ghost hunter called Tony Cornell.

Most investigators simply go to wherever it is that they believe to be haunted, set up all their cameras, microphones, tripwires and other gubbins and then sit back and wait – and wait. It's a bit like fishing . . . only without any bait. Nothing of any real interest has come forward from these investigations. This either means that ghosts are camera-shy, or that they need an actual real live human in the room, or that they really are only in the imagination of the onlooker. Most proper scientists don't believe in ghosts, therefore, because there's no real scientific way of studying them.

Ghost Tricksters

There are some weirdos, however, who take it much further. They get so caught up in the whole ghastly ghostly business that they form sort of Ghost clubs, dashing off for long weekends to seek ghosts. These people hang around old houses and spooky places with special equipment in order to try and trick the ghosts into revealing themselves. The trouble is, just like the people who go out looking for UFOs, some of them fiddle around with the evidence, for reasons best known to themselves, just to fool us.

Ghostly Ways

If you are still determined to try ghost hunting, there are a few things you might need to know.

According to the experts, most ghosts are a pretty aimless bunch, simply drifting around with no real purpose. Having said that, if the ghost in question belongs to a relative or friend, they often try to make contact. Usually the ghosts don't seem to know or care if real people are around. They tend to stick to houses rather than humans.

Ghosts aren't much good at conversation. If they do talk, they tend to get it over with quickly. And because they're not actually made of anything, they tend to be pretty harmless. Therefore, most people will survive being punched by a ghost . . . unless they die of fright. We live people are only really scared of them because we don't know what they are.

Some ghosts, however, can cause a bit of physical grief, like in the story of the vicar's wife at Elm Vicarage, Wisbech, Cambridgeshire, who was rescued by one ghost from being throttled by another (a monk ghost, as it happens). She carried real live bruises on her neck for ages.

What to do if you see a ghost

If you go out hunting with a group of mates, and you happen to end up in the presence of a ghost, only one of you will see it. If you do happen to be the chosen one, this is what you should do.

1 Keep completely still. Don't move a muscle – you might frighten it away.

2 If the ghost speaks to you, be very polite. Ask it its name and age, what sex it is (if you can't see) and what it's come back for (to see old friends, scare the life out of someone, check what's happened in Coronation Street etc, etc.)

3 Ask if it's in any sort of trouble and if it is, see if there's anything you can do to help.

4 Invite the ghost to come back again, but make sure you get it to say what time and where it will be arriving, otherwise you could be standing around in the dark for ever.

5 Wait until the ghost moves before you do. If it leaves

through an open door, try following. But if the door's closed take care not to injure yourself. If at all possible, nip round to see what's on the other side.

Ghost Busters

If you have a bad ghost you want rid of, you will find that most vicars perform services called *exorcisms*. Apparently you only have to give the local church a ring and they'll send someone round to flush 'em out – a bit like like Dyno-Rod do for blocked pipes – except ghost removal's free!

Home Exorcism in Ten Easy Stages

(By the way, make sure the person doing it has no naughty habits or dark secrets, otherwise the evil spirit might jump across to him.)

1 Do it somewhere where there's a connection between the demon and the victim – like a bedroom.

2 Gather together some salt (representing purity), red wine (representing the blood of Christ) and a bucket of holy water.

3 Give the victim a cross to hold and maybe some bones of a saint (if you happen to have any in the house).

4 Try to find out the identity of the actual demon. It is most important.

5 Recite as many biblical scriptures and prayers as you can think of.

6 Breakpoint! When the demon finally gives in, be prepared for pandemonium and a load of foul language and even worse smells. The demon usually turns on the

victim and abuses him, using the victim's own voice.

7   Silence the demon's voice in order to continue.

8   As his voice dies out, one may feel a spiritual and physical pressure. The demon has collided with the 'will of the kingdom', and is in direct conflict with the exorcist.

9   The demon is now looking for somewhere to go. He most certainly doesn't want to go home to Hell, however.

10 In a triumph of God's will, the exorcist dismisses the spirit in the name of Jesus. Everyone present feels great relief.

11 Nobody present may have any secret sins, for, as he leaves, the demon will shout them out for all to hear and probably ruin the exorcism.

THE BITTER END

Just in case you're in any way tempted to throw a sheet over your head just before bedtime and scare your brother or sister half to death, take heed of this little story.

The Greek scholar Erasmus tells of a very rich and good-looking lady who witnessed a ghost in her bedchamber. Instead of running, she grabbed a big stick and beat the living daylights out of what turned out to be a man hiding under a sheet trying to scare her – 'until he screamed out for mercy'.

Well I hope you've now got a better picture of ghosts after reading this book, although I'm not sure whether you'll believe in them more now you've got to the end, or less. Personally, the only way I'd really believe in ghosts is if I met one myself. So far I haven't, but I've come pretty close. Many years ago I revisited a small hotel on a cliffside in South Devon that I'd once stayed at. It was locked up and deserted. I left my girlfriend at the front while I had a look around. As I was strolling back I could hear her talking. I asked her whom she'd met and she was surprised that I hadn't seen the couple of old ladies who'd told her they were the owners. There was no sign of them and you could see for miles around.

That evening, in the local pub, we learned that a year ago the two sisters who had run the place had tragically died within two months of each other and the hotel was now up for sale.

Anyway, that's the end of my little history of ghosts. Although, when pressed, I'm still not sure they really exist, nothing in the world could persuade me to spend the night in a lonely graveyard. How's about you?

By the way, what's that dark shape looming just behind you?

THE SHORT AND

BLOODY

HISTORY

OF

All aboard, Landlubbers!

PIRATES

John Farman

Have you ever wondered why pirates wore gold earrings, or where the saying 'sick as a parrot' came from? And do you know who the cruellest pirate in history was?
John Farman's got all the answers, so come aboard for his short and bloody history of the day-to-day life of pirates!

£2.99   0 09 940709 4

THE SHORT AND
BLOODY
HISTORY
OF

Call me
Inspector!

SPIES

John Farman

Psst! Do you know how to make invisible
ink or send a coded message? And have
you heard about the pope who was a spy?
John Farman's been doing some spying of his
own and has uncovered all the answers in this
fantastic book. But beware, this message will
self-destruct in five seconds!

£2.99   0 09 940715 9

THE SHORT AND
BLOODY
HISTORY
OF

Fancy a joust?

KNIGHTS

John Farman

Have you ever wondered how knights managed to walk, let alone fight, covered from head
to foot in metal? And have you heard about the
knights who became addicted to jousting?
Or the one who was rescued by a monkey?
It's all in John Farman's brilliant book.
So arm yourself for a
fact attack!

£2.99   0 09 940712

The Very Bloody History of London

By John Farman

WITHOUT THE BORING BITS

When a man is tired of London, he is tired of life... **Samuel Johnson**

Let John Farman, author of the mega-bestselling title *The Very Bloody History of Britain,* guide you round one of the world's most famous cities, London. Packed with a multitude of facts to entertain and amaze you, *The Very Bloody History of London* will take you on a tour you will never forget. Sometimes grisly, but always fascinating, this is history as it should be — loads of fun!

John Farman
THE VERY BLOODY HISTORY OF LONDON
Red Fox paperback, £3.99, ISBN 0 09 940412 5